21st Century
Skills Library

REAL WORLD MATH: PERSONAL FINANCE

Smart Shopping

Cecilia Minden

Discard
NHCPL

New Hanover County Public Library
201 Chestnut Street
Wilmington, NC 28401

Published in the United States of America by Cherry Lake Publishing
Ann Arbor, MI
www.cherrylakepublishing.com

Math Education Adviser: Timothy J. Whiteford, PhD, Associate Professor of Education, St. Michael's College, Colchester, Vermont

Finance Adviser: Ryan Spaude, CFP®, Kitchenmaster Financial Services, LLC, North Mankato, Minnesota

Copyright ©2008 by Cherry Lake Publishing
All rights reserved. No part of this book may be reproduced or utilized in any form or by any means without written permission from the publisher.

Cherry Lake Publishing would like to acknowledge the work of
The Partnership for 21st Century Skills.
Please visit www.21stcenturyskills.org for more information.

TABLE OF CONTENTS

CHAPTER ONE
The Mall and More   4

CHAPTER TWO
I Need That!   8

CHAPTER THREE
Do the Math: How Much Will It Cost?   13

CHAPTER FOUR
Do the Math: Paying for Your Purchase   18

CHAPTER FIVE
Be a Smart Shopper   24

Real World Math Challenge Answers   29

Glossary   30

For More Information   31

Index   32

About the Author   32

THE MALL AND MORE

In some communities, farmers sell their fruits and vegetables at a weekly farmer's market.

Have you ever traded sports cards or CDs with a friend? If so, you were **bartering**. Long ago, people used bartering as a way to trade what they could make or grow for what they wanted. Bartering was the first method of shopping. Sometimes people bartered a service such as helping each other build a barn or cabin. Sometimes they bartered crops or handcrafted items. Each week, farmers brought goods for sale into town. Rural families would gather to sell and trade their goods. It was a social event that gave families a chance to spend time with their friends.

Eventually, permanent shops replaced the markets. Goods came from bigger cities. Shops often specialized in one product. A shopper could buy bread from the bakery, books from the bookshop, or shoes from the cobbler. A shopper gave a list to the shopkeeper, who fetched items from the shelves. Some shop owners would even deliver goods to people's homes.

As populations grew, so did the need for more goods and faster service. Specialty shops grouped together to make shopping easier for the customer. They became department stores and supermarkets. Shoppers picked out their own **merchandise**. The idea of "self-service" was

promoted as a way to save money and time.

Families began to move away from the cities and into the **suburbs**.

They wanted stores near their homes. Malls gave shoppers the convenience

of a nearby place to shop, more choices of stores, and places to park. The

first shopping mall was called The Plaza. It opened in Kansas City, Kansas,

in 1922. Mall of America, the most visited mall in the United States, opened in Bloomington, Minnesota, in 1992. It has more than 500 shops, an amusement

The Plaza shopping mall is now known as the Country Club Plaza and is a 15-block shopping and entertainment district.

6

park, an aquarium, and a dinosaur park museum!

Much like the markets of old, shopping centers

provide a place for friends to gather and spend

time together.

The newest way to shop is on the Internet.

Thousands of Web sites provide shoppers with

choices from around the world. Customers can even

barter for items on the Internet. As new ways of

shopping become popular, the old ways continue.

With so many choices, how can you become a

smart shopper? How do you decide where and what

to buy? How can you get the best price for your

purchase? Let's find out!

You can shop for masks from Africa, sweaters from Ireland, or guitars from Brazil without ever leaving your home. The Internet makes it easy to access goods from all over the world and have them delivered to your home.

CHAPTER TWO

I Need That!

"But everybody has one!" Have you heard or said those words before?

A smart shopper can tell the difference between wanting and needing.

If you have rows of shirts in your closet, you probably have more shirts than you need.

Needing something means you have to have it to complete a task or goal. We *need* to wear clothing to protect us from the weather. The kind of clothing we *want* and how much we spend is a choice. Sometimes you can find something you really like for a great price. That is the work of a smart shopper!

Let's say you are going on vacation and need to figure out what clothes you will take with you. Where should you begin? The first place to shop is your room! Go through closets, drawers, and shelves. What needs to

Learning & Innovation Skills

Deciding between what you want and what you need can be a great way to exercise your reasoning skills and learn how to make choices. You will want to consider as many different points of view as you possibly can. For instance, let's say you are thinking about buying a new swimsuit for your trip. Ask yourself some questions. For example:

- Do I already have a swimsuit that still fits? If I do, do I really need another one?
- If I don't have a swimsuit, do I have to buy one or can I borrow one?
- Am I certain that I will be going swimming on my vacation?

You may end up going out to buy a new swimsuit after all, but at least you will be sure that it is what you *really* want or need to do.

It is a good idea to make a list of what you need and figure out how much money you have to spend before you go shopping.

be replaced and what can be cleaned or repaired? As you work, keep track of what you need to buy in a small notebook. Glue an envelope in the back to hold coupons and discount tickets. Keeping a record will help you compare prices and make the best choices.

Before you go shopping, go through your list. What do you need to buy now? Are there things on the list that would be nice to have but are not necessary for the trip? Include a cost estimate for each item. Do some online research at stores' Web sites to get a realistic idea of prices and quality. Be sure to check different stores carrying the same items. The mall

Checking prices online can help you save time and money.

may be your first choice but also check out discount stores and outlet stores. Comparing prices ahead of time saves time and money.

You know what you want to buy, but what if you don't have enough money? The best plan is to postpone the shopping trip until you can pay for what you need. That way, you can really enjoy the new item, knowing it is all yours. Can't wait? Before you borrow from parents or siblings, be sure you all agree on how you will pay back the money. They won't want to keep reminding you, and you won't want to hear them nagging you!

REAL WORLD MATH CHALLENGE

Mike saved up $15.00 for a new basketball. Super Sports has the one he wants for $18.00. Al's Athletics sells the same basketball for $20.00, but it is on sale for 15 percent off through the end of the month. Sales tax is 5 percent.

Which store has the lower price? How much more money does Mike need to buy that basketball at the store with the lower price?

(Turn to page 29 for the answers)

CHAPTER THREE

DO THE MATH:
HOW MUCH WILL IT COST?

You know what you want and how much you have to spend. How can

you get the best price for what you want to buy?

One way is to wait for sales. At certain times of the year, stores offer

you a bigger discount. January is a great time for after-holiday sales.

*Waiting until items you want go on sale is a good strategy
for getting the most merchandise for your money.*

You may find some good bargains if you spend some time searching through the crowded racks at a discount store.

Winter clothing often goes on sale in February, and July is a good time to find bargains on summer clothes. Stores need to make room for newer, seasonal merchandise. Get in the habit of searching local newspapers and store Web sites to check sale prices. The end of every season is a good time to search the store for items to use the following year.

A shopping mall visit may be fun, but other stores may offer you a better price. *Discount stores* buy merchandise in large quantities to be able to offer lower prices. Check at the entrance to see if they offer a map of the store so you can find what you are looking for quickly. If you start to wander around, you may end up buying something you don't really need! If an item isn't on the shelf, ask a salesperson if there might be another one in the storeroom. Don't be discouraged if the discount stores seem too big or cluttered. If you have the patience to search carefully, you might find just what you are looking for.

21st Century Content

One of the oldest and most famous discount store chains in the United States is Filene's Basement. The chain was founded in Boston, Massachusetts, in 1909. Each year, the store in Boston holds an event called the "running of the brides." Crowds of women all rush into the store at the same time trying to find a great price on a wedding dress. Why does the store do this? The event gets a lot of publicity and brings more shoppers into the store.

Taking the time to look for coupons in newspapers and online can help you save money on the things you want to buy.

Outlet stores sell name brands at reduced costs. Merchandise is

frequently off-season or slightly damaged. With a little effort, you can get

popular brands at bargain prices. Sometimes outlet stores cluster together

to form an outlet mall.

Coupons are another way to save. Invented in 1895, coupons were first used to promote a new soft drink, Coca-Cola. More than 100 years later, The Coca-Cola Company is still offering coupons to sell its products! It is important to read coupons carefully. Sometimes **restrictions** may apply. Be sure to check the **expiration date** on the coupon. Smart shoppers do their math to decide if a discount at one store or a coupon at another will give them the best price.

Now you've made your list, checked out prices, and gathered coupons. What else do you need to consider?

REAL WORLD MATH CHALLENGE

Beth is shopping for a new sweater. She has $25.00 to spend. She found a coupon for 20 percent off one item at Cook's Department Store in the newspaper. The coupon can't be used for items that are on sale. At the store, Beth found a pretty blue sweater for $22.95. She also found a pretty green sweater on sale for $19.99. **Which sweater will cost less? How much less?**

(Turn to page 29 for the answers)

CHAPTER FOUR

DO THE MATH:
PAYING FOR YOUR PURCHASE

*Most states have a sales tax that is charged when
you buy food, clothing and other items.*

You found what you were looking for at a great price. What other costs

should you consider? Nearly all states charge a sales tax, but these taxes

differ from state to state. Massachusetts, for example, doesn't charge sales tax on clothing but does charge sales tax on other items. The amount of

tax charged will also depend on what you buy. You may pay a higher tax on

luxury items such as televisions or expensive clothing. Necessities, such as

food or medical items, may have a lower tax or none at all.

REAL WORLD MATH CHALLENGE

Sales tax is a percentage of the basic price of an item. Let's say you go to the grocery store to buy treats for a class party. Your purchase comes to $19.62. State and local taxes total 7 percent. You have $20.00 to spend. **Do you have enough money to pay for your purchase? Add the purchase price and taxes to find out what the item really costs.**

(Turn to page 29 for the answer)

It is a good idea to take a pocket calculator with you when you shop.

You can total up your items and figure taxes before you get to the cash

register, to make sure you have enough money. The calculator is also handy for comparing prices. Another quick way to add sums is to round

up and get an estimate of what something will cost. Instead of calculating

exact amounts, take the numbers up to the next whole number. It is easier

Taking a small calculator with you when you go
shopping can help you stay within your budget.

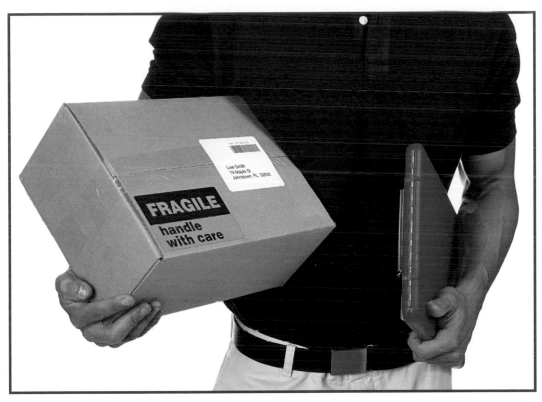

You need to add shipping charges to the cost of the item you are buying when you shop online or phone in a catalog order.

to figure 5 percent of $20.00 than 5 percent of $19.88, if you don't have a

calculator handy.

If you are buying items from another city or state, you will usually

have to pay for the store to ship it to you. Shipping costs depend on where

21st Century Content

State and local taxes help to pay for things everyone in a community can share, such as schools, parks, highways, and libraries.

the item is located and where and how you want it shipped. Other factors include package weight and how quickly you want to receive the item. Sometimes there are special handling costs such as extra packing for fragile items or perishable foods. Some stores have a minimum amount for shipping costs. This means you have to spend a certain amount before they will send a package to you. Stores frequently offer special deals giving you free shipping if your items cost more than a certain amount. You can also see if they will ship it to a nearby branch store. Companies sometimes offer free shipping if you can pick up the order at their local store.

Accidents can result in unexpected expenses!

REAL WORLD MATH CHALLENGE

Lorenzo and Kiera accidentally broke Mom's favorite vase. They searched online and found one just like it for $15.00. Tax is 7 percent, and shipping costs are $2.99 plus $0.59 per pound. The vase weighs 2 pounds. They tell their mom that they want to give her the money so she can order the vase online.

How much money do Lorenzo and Kiera need to replace the broken vase? If Lorenzo and Kiera agree to split the cost evenly, how much do they each have to contribute toward the cost of the vase?

(Turn to page 29 for the answers)

CHAPTER FIVE

BE A SMART SHOPPER

Shopping with friends can be fun.

You've made a list, compared prices, gathered coupons, and set aside extra cash for taxes. A few more tips will help make your shopping trip the best ever.

Get an early start to avoid long lines. The largest crowds are usually between midmorning and late afternoon. Wear comfortable shoes. Dress in layers so you won't get too hot or too cold. Be sure to carry money in a secure pocket or purse. It is fun to shop with a group of friends or family members, but you don't want to spend all of your time looking for one another. Make sure you have a plan for what to do if you get separated.

Maybe you prefer to shop online. The Internet is convenient, and you can find some great deals. But there are guidelines to follow to make a safe purchase. You need to compare and consider Web offers just as you would in any store.

Shopping with a group of family members or friends can be a test of your problem-solving skills and flexibility. You'll all have to work together to come up with a plan that lets everyone shop for what he or she wants. You will also have to make sure that nobody gets separated from the entire group. A good plan can be to split up into smaller groups that want to go to the same stores. Decide on a time and place for everyone to meet for the trip home. Being flexible and making sure everyone has a good time can make the day more pleasant for everyone.

A general rule to follow is that if something sounds too good to be true, then it probably is. Check a Web site thoroughly and get an adult's permission before entering any personal information, especially information that gives the Web site access to a bank account or credit cards. You should never have to reveal your Social Security number.

If you do get adult permission to make a purchase, how can you tell that the Web site is secure and will protect your personal information? Look for a padlock **icon** on your screen. That is one indication you are on a secure site that will protect your information. Another way to tell, according to Leslie Hunt of Bankrate.com, is that the letters *http* in the **URL** should change to *https*. Remember, always check with an adult before making any online purchase. They may be able to help you avoid an online shopping disaster.

Smart shopping is fun. It is like a game or mystery. You put together

all the clues and figure out the best way to solve the puzzle. Saving money

means you can either buy more or put the money you save aside for

Always check with a parent before buying anything online.

another day. Smart shoppers can really enjoy new purchases when they

know that they put in the time and effort necessary to get what they really

wanted at a price they could afford.

Let's go shopping!

REAL WORLD MATH CHALLENGE

Larry received $45.00 for his birthday. He earned $75.00 mowing lawns. He wants to buy a rack to hold all of his CDs, but he also wants to buy a new computer game and a DVD. He searched several places online and found that Tena's Tent of Values has the best prices for all of those products, but Computer Cabin doesn't charge for shipping if your order total is more than $100.00.

The rack at Tena's Tent of Values costs $41.99 and will hold 250 CDs. The shipping costs are $14.75.

Computer Cabin has a better-quality rack for $61.88 that also holds 250 CDs. He has a coupon for 15 percent off one item at Computer Cabin.

At both places, the computer game is $39.95, and the DVD is $19.95. There is a 5 percent sales tax on the total.

What would Larry's total cost be at Tena's Tent of Values? At Computer Cabin? Does Larry have enough money for everything?

(Turn to page 29 for the answers)

REAL WORLD MATH CHALLENGE ANSWERS

Chapter Two
Page 12

The basketball at Al's Athletics is on sale at 15 percent off of $20.00.

$.15 \times \$20.00 = \$3.00$

$\$20.00 - \$3.00 = \$17.00$

The price of the basketball at Al's Athletics is $17.00. At Super Sports, it costs $18.00. Al's Athletics has the lower price.

Now the 5 percent sales tax needs to be added in.

$.05 \times \$17.00 = \$0.85$

$\$17.00 + \$0.85 = \$17.85$

This is the total cost of the basketball. Mike only has $15.00.

$\$17.85 - \$15.00 = \$2.85$

Mike needs $2.85 more to be able to purchase the basketball.

Chapter Three
Page 17

A coupon for 20 percent off would work on the blue sweater, which costs $22.95.

$.20 \times \$22.95 = \$4.59$

$\$22.95 - \$4.59 = \$18.36$

The coupon lowers the price of the blue sweater to $18.36.

The price of the green sweater is $19.99.

$\$19.99 - \$18.36 = \$1.63$

The blue sweater costs $1.63 less than the green sweater.

Chapter Four
Page 19

Treats purchased at the grocery store total $19.62. State and local taxes total 7 percent.

$.07 \times \$19.62 = \$1.38$

$\$19.62 + \$1.38 = \$21.00$

With only $20.00, you don't have enough money. You are short by $1.00.

Page 23

The vase is $15.00 plus 7 percent sales tax.

$.07 \times \$15.00 = \$1.05$

The tax will be $1.05.

The vase weighs 2 pounds, and part of the shipping charge is $0.59 per pound.

$2 \times \$0.59 = \$1.18$

The rest of the shipping charge is $2.99.

$\$2.99 + \$1.18 = \$4.17$

The total shipping cost will be $4.17.

To replace the broken vase, it will cost:

$\$15.00 + \$1.05 + \$4.17 = \$20.22$

Lorenzo and Kiera agree to split the cost evenly.

$\$20.22 \div 2 = \$10.11$

Lorenzo and Kiera each need to give Mom $10.11.

Chapter Five
Page 28

At Tena's Tent of Values, the price of the three items is:

$\$41.99 + \$39.95 + \$19.95 = \$101.89$

There is a 5 percent sales tax on the total.

$.05 \times \$101.89 = \$5.09$

The total of the items, the sales tax, and the shipping is:

$\$101.89 + \$5.09 + \$14.75 = \$121.73$

At Computer Cabin, the 15 percent off coupon is good on the $61.88 CD rack.

$.15 \times \$61.88 = \$9.28$

$\$61.88 - \$9.28 = \$52.60$

The price of the three items is:

$\$52.60 + \$39.95 + \$19.95 = \$112.50$

There is a 5 percent sales tax on the total.

$.05 \times \$112.50 = \$5.63$

The total of the items and the sales tax is (there is no shipping charge because the order totals more than $100.00):

$\$112.50 + \$5.63 = \$118.13$

Larry has $120.00.

$\$45.00 + \$75.00 = \$120.00$

If he buys all three items at Computer Cabin, which costs less than Tena's, he will have $1.87 left.

$\$120.00 - \$118.13 = \$1.87$

Glossary

bartering (BAR-tur-ing) trading or exchanging one good or service for another instead of using money

expiration date (ek-spuh-RAY-shuhn dayt) the date when something, such as a coupon, is no longer valid

icon (I-kon) a picture that represents something

merchandise (MURR-chuhn-dice) goods that are bought or sold

restrictions (rih-STRIK-shuhnz) limitations on the use of something

suburbs (SUB-urbz) residential areas on the outskirts of a city or large town

URL (yu-ar-EL) the address of a Web site on the Internet; stands for uniform resource locator or universal resource locator

FOR MORE INFORMATION

Books

Burkett, Lauree , Christie Bowler, and Chris Kielesinski (illustrator).
Money Matters for Kids. Chicago: Moody Press, 1997.

Holyoke, Nancy, and Ali Douglass (illustrator). *A Smart Girl's Guide to Money:
How to Make It, Save It, and Spend It*. Middleton, WI: American Girl, 2006.

Web Sites

Internal Revenue Service—Understanding Taxes
www.irs.gov/app/understandingTaxes/jsp/s_student_home.jsp
Information and activities that help you learn more about taxes

Maryland Public Television—Sense and Dollars
http://senseanddollars.thinkport.org/
For games that teach money management skills

INDEX

bank accounts, 26
Bankrate Web site, 26
bartering, 4–5
Bloomington, Minnesota, 6
borrowing, 9, 12
Boston, Massachusetts, 15

calculators, 19–21
Coca-Cola Company, 17
coupons, 10, 16–17, 24, 28
credit cards, 26
crowds, 15, 25

department stores, 5–6
discount stores, 12, 15
discount tickets, 10

expiration dates, 17

Filene's Basement, 15
free shipping, 22

handling costs, 22
Hunt, Leslie, 26

Internet, 7, 11, 25–27, 28

Kansas City, Kansas, 6

local taxes, 19, 22
luxury items, 19

Mall of America, 6–7
Massachusetts, 18–19
merchandise, 6, 14, 15, 16

needs, 8–9, 11

outlet stores, 12, 16

padlock icons, 26
planning, 25
The Plaza, 6

research, 11
restrictions, 17

sales, 12, 13–14, 17
sales tax, 12, 18–19, 28

savings, 6, 12, 16, 27–28
shipping costs, 21–22, 23, 28
shopping malls, 6–7, 11–12,
   15, 16
shops, 5, 6
Social Security numbers, 26
specialty shops, 5
state taxes, 19, 22
suburbs, 6
supermarkets, 5–6

taxes, 12, 18–19, 22, 24, 28

wants, 8, 9, 11
Web sites, 7, 11, 14, 25–26,

ABOUT THE AUTHOR

Cecilia Minden, PhD, is a literacy consultant and the author of many books for children. She is the former director of the Language and Literacy Program at Harvard Graduate School of Education in Cambridge, Massachusetts. She would like to thank fifth-grade math teacher Beth Rottinghaus for her help with the Real World Math Challenges. Cecilia lives with her family in North Carolina.